# *Practical Guide*
## *for Internal Consultants*

*Using Your Expertise to Build Business Capacity*

**james d. showkeir**
henning-showkeir & associates

**kevin herring**
ascent management consulting

*h-s associates*

# Practical Guide for Internal Consultants

This book was created as a collaboration of James D. Showkeir of Henning-Showkeir & Associates and Kevin Herring of Ascent Management Consulting, Ltd. It is grounded in the work of Joel P. Henning who saw the potential for staff groups to add significantly greater value to core business units.

## Henning-Showkeir & Associates

7 Mohawk Trail
Westfield, NJ 07090
**Phone:** (908) 232-9994
**Fax:** (908) 389-0211
**E-Mail:** homeoffice@henning-showkeir.com
**Web site:** http://www.henning-showkeir.com

## Ascent Management Consulting, Ltd.

330 E. Glenhurst Drive
Oro Valley, AZ 85704
**Phone:** (520) 742-7300
**Fax:** (520) 742-9236
**E-Mail:** info@ascentmgt.com
**Web site:** http://www.ascentmgt.com

ISBN 0-9764301-0-X
Library of Congress Control Number 2004117522
Printed in the United States of America

First Edition
10 9 8 7 6 5 4 3 2

Cover Design by David Payne

## This book is dedicated to Joel...

We thank Joel Henning for inspiring this work and creating the foundation principles for which staff professionals everywhere are reaping the benefit. His imprint is apparent throughout this handbook.

For over 30 years Joel was engaged in complex long-term organizational change efforts. His work spanned a broad range of organizations from public school systems facing desegregation to large corporations reinventing their futures in the face of changing marketplaces and competition.

Out of this change work came the realization that an organization's capacity to navigate change and succeed is determined by its willingness to develop individuals through the intentional distribution of power—business literacy, choice, purpose and accountability.

He authored *The Future of Staff Groups: Daring to Distribute Power and Capacity* published by Berrett-Koehler.

Joel passed away unexpectedly in May of 2001. His book and *henning-showkeir & associates* are part of his legacy.

We hope this work does justice to that legacy.

# Acknowledgments

Thanks to Jayne Sanford whose thoroughness and eye for detail saved us from our oversights, sloppiness, and blurry-eyed sign offs. Jayne remains the backbone of the *henning-showkeir & associates* organization.

Many thanks to Brian Bub for the use of his *fine tooth comb* in identifying the opportunities for improving this work. His enthusiasm for contributing, incredible professional versatility, and difficulty saying "no" make him a welcomed addition to any team.

Thanks to all of the staff professionals who were willing to plow through the first extremely rough draft. Their valuable insights and encouragement to pursue the project helped us persevere in creating what we saw as a beginning for moving this work forward.

Thanks to all the staff people willing to take the risk of reinventing themselves as internal consultants who are dedicated to building business capacity and ensuring the success of core business units.

# Contents

# About This Book...

In 1997, Joel Henning's revolutionary new book *The Future of Staff Groups: Daring to Distribute Power and Capacity* was published. Since that time, many organizations have successfully applied these powerful principles in Human Resources, Information Systems, Accounting, Purchasing, Finance, Engineering and other staff groups.

As a result, these staff groups are beginning to create convincing results for the core business. They have reinvented themselves as internal consulting businesses that utilize staff expertise in resolving core business issues. Their expertise is responsible for improving profitability, quality, cycle time and unique customer response.

This guide is developed as a complement to Henning's book. It provides practical summaries of concepts, tools, applications and models for staff individuals and groups. It may be used as a stand-alone guide for powerful consulting, or as a field reference for *The Future of Staff Groups*. It is most useful to staff people dedicated to proving their worth both to their clients in the core business and their bankers to whom they have made substantive promises.

This is a *handbook*. A complete explanation of principles and concepts can be found in *The Future of Staff Groups* although brief explanations are provided throughout this book. This book is designed as a reference with applications, tools and reminders.

**Charts and tools are provided throughout. Feel free to copy and enlarge them. USE THEM as practical resources in your development and contribution to your core business.**

Those in staff positions should find this reference useful for becoming powerful internal consultants in any organization. Please consider this book for all those in your organization who serve the core business in some way.

We encourage you to contact us and share your experiences using the material. We welcome your comments and suggestions.

# Chapter One

## Consulting Basics

# Definitions

**BANKER** – Responsible for providing assets (i.e. budgets, resources) to staff groups and the core business in exchange for a promise.

**BUILDING CAPACITY** – Using staff group expertise for improving the *concurrent* management of quality, profitability, cycle time, and unique customer response.

**CAPACITY** – Concurrently managing quality, profitability, cycle time, unique customer response.

**CLIENT** – Those in core work processes producing products or delivering services to customers and departments, or those groups generating revenue for the business (i.e. the core business).

**CONSULTANT** – Internal support services staff person dedicated to serving the core business.

**CORE BUSINESS** – Department or work area producing products, delivering services, or performing functions to generate revenue according to the organization's mission (i.e. Operations).

**CORE WORKER** – Employee directly involved in processes that produce products, deliver services, or generate revenue.

**EXPERTISE** – Theories, knowledge, skills, abilities, competencies and experience.

**FIT** – Agreement between consultant recommendations and client *willingness* to implement them.

**GUARANTEE** – Security for delivering on a promise made by a consultant to a client or banker.

**MANAGEMENT PRACTICES** – Rules, policies and procedures to control employee behavior and create governance in the organization.

**OFFER** – Proposal of a business solution a consultant presents to a client and a marketplace.

**ORGANIZATION ARCHITECTURE** – The systems that arrange people, functions and assigned rewards.

**ORGANIZATIONAL POWER** – Business literacy, choice and decision making, accountability for the whole, access and allocation of resources, and the competence to manage and do the work are the elements of organizational power.

**PROMISE** – A commitment to deliver a specified outcome made by a consultant to a client or banker.

**RELEVANCE** – Agreement between consultant expertise and what is necessary to build client capacity.

**SOCIAL CONTRACT** (CULTURE) – How the individual and organization relate to one another.

**STAFF GROUP** – Support services function (i.e. Human Resources, Purchasing, Training, Information Systems, Accounting, Finance) providing support to the core business.

**STANCE** – Consultant point of view about how consulting expertise should be applied in client organization.

**TIMELINESS** – Appropriateness of point in time for implementing consultant recommendations.

# Concept

**Principles of Effective Consulting:**

√ Consultant's initiatives are driven by marketplace demands that require increased client capacity

√ Client has choice regarding whether or not to accept consultant offers

√ Consultant promises to build client capacity in the marketplace

√ Consultant backs promises with something significant at stake — a guarantee

√ Consultant accomplishes critical objectives of each stage of consulting

√ Consultant operates from a decided stance regarding how personal expertise is used in client organization

√ Consultant operates with integrity regarding ethical issues of honesty, nondiscrimination, confidentiality, etc.

√ Consultant uses expertise to directly impact quality, profitability, cycle time and unique customer response in client organization

√ Consultant assesses relevance, timeliness and fit of expertise in client organization, and accepts assignment when assessment supports success

√ Consultant gives direct feedback with goodwill to client about client's contribution to organization issues

**Tool**

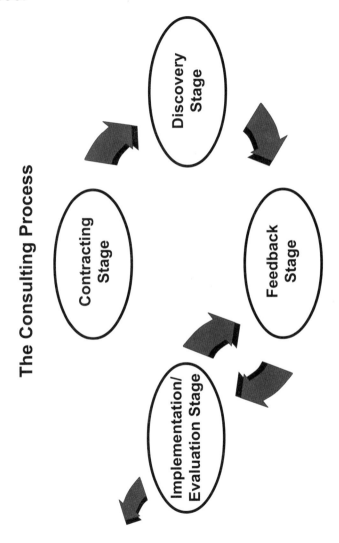

The Consulting Process

Discovery Stage

Contracting Stage

Feedback Stage

Implementation/ Evaluation Stage

# Stages of the Consulting Process

**Stage 1: Contracting**
- Establish the consulting relationship
- Establish conditions that allow you to assess relevance, timeliness and fit of consultant expertise
- Reach explicit agreement with client on conditions for proceeding

**Stage 2: Discovery**
- Gather data about the business/technical and management/personal aspects of the situation
- Collect information from people throughout the business unit about relevance, timeliness and fit of consultant expertise

**Stage 3: Feedback**

*Phase 1 - Resolving Fit and Implementation Decisions*
- Determine how you will begin to apply your expertise to help build capacity in the unit
- Establish conditions client must create for successful implementation
- Present the client with the major issues about relevance, timeliness and fit of consultant expertise
- Determine business outcomes to be achieved (i.e. quality, profitability, cycle time and unique response)
- Reach *go/no go* decision

*Phase 2 - Contracting for Ongoing Implementation*
- Develop project plan with deliverables
- Establish process for measuring success
- Determine milestones and individual actions

**Stage 4: Implementation/Evaluation**
- Continuously assess and recontract as necessary
- Establish successful completion, re-contracting, or termination of implementation

# Application

## Consulting Orientation Self Assessment

*The following assessment will help you contrast traditional consulting models with the model presented here:*

1. *Purpose* - What should be the primary objective of most consulting projects?

   a. build core business unit capacity

   b. satisfy corporate staff objectives

The primary objective of most consulting projects should be to directly build the capacity of the core business to improve the bottom line by reducing costs, increasing sales, improving productivity and quality, satisfying customers, reducing response times, providing a unique response to the customer, etc.

2. *Initial Contracting* - What should be the outcome of the initial client meeting?

   a. identify project scope and resource requirements

   b. create conditions to assess relevance, timeliness and fit of consultant's expertise

The outcome of the initial client meeting is to establish conditions you, as the consultant, and the client need to determine the relevance, timeliness and fit of your expertise – i.e. is your expertise useful?

3. *Discovery* - What should you as a consultant gain by gathering your own information?

a. can validate the client's view of the problem

b. can determine if your own expertise is relevant

By collecting your own data, you can obtain a clear picture as to whether or not your expertise is relevant, timely and fits. You must make this determination for yourself. You may, or may not, validate the client's perception.

4. *Feedback* - What should you as a consultant disclose to the client when presenting feedback?

a. difficult issues including those involving the client

b. only issues falling within the scope of the project

You should disclose to the client all the difficult issues that must be resolved in order to fulfill your promise to the client. Failing to do so is a disservice to the client. Your feedback should include the client's contribution to the problem and directly confront the fit issues.

5. *Contracting for Implementation* - Who should assume responsibility for implementing recommendations?

   a. the client because only the client knows what will work in the business unit

   b. the consultant as the one who prescribed the solution

In most cases, the answer is both. You as the consultant must collaborate with the client for successful implementation. Merely handing off recommendations will leave you with the accountability for outcomes and no ability to influence them. Success requires both parties applying their expertise, working together and owning the outcome.

6. *Implementation* - What is the best criteria for determining successful implementation?

   a. activities completed on time and within budget

   b. increased capacity / improved business results

Success is determined by improvement in an organization's capacity to manage marketplace demands. An effective implementation should directly impact quality, profitability, cycle time, and/or customer response.

# Chapter Two

## Defining Expertise

# Concept

**Defining Expertise for Client Value**

Consultant must possess expertise:

√ that is relevant to the business

√ that is complex, deep and not easily mastered

√ that changes rapidly, requires focused attention

√ that is essential, but infrequently used or held in reserve

Fundamental components of consultant **EXPERTISE**:

*Knowledge*
*Skills*
*Abilities*  } = **EXPERTISE**
*Competencies*
*Experience*

**TECHNIQUES, MODELS, METHODS AND ACTIVITIES ARE APPLICATIONS OF EXPERTISE**

**Examples of**
*TECHNIQUES, MODELS, METHODS AND ACTIVITIES*

- √ Developing training programs

- √ Troubleshooting computer problems

- √ Analyzing financial data

- √ Creating contract specifications

- √ Auditing financial reports

- √ Facilitating group processes

- √ Developing computer code

- √ Negotiating agreements

- √ Conducting surveys

- √ Reconfiguring hardware

- √ Planning cash flow strategy

- √ Work flow diagramming

## Examples of Internal Consultant *EXPERTISE*

**Information Systems**:
The retrieval, manipulation and distribution of information.

**Finance**:
The creation and interpretation of key measures for business decision-making.

**Human Resources**:
The definition, organization and maximization of individual and group contributions to achieve specific goals and objectives.

**Training**:
The creation of learning solutions focused on specific business problems.

**Purchasing**:
The creation of supplier partnerships that increase business capacity.

**Manufacturing Engineering**:
The development of process solutions to exceed customer and business output requirements.

## To add value consultant expertise must impact

√ Profitability/Cost
√ Quality
√ Cycle Time
√ Unique Responses to Marketplace Demands

## The critical question:

*What do you or your staff group know how to do that you believe yields powerful business results?*

# Application

*Define your own expertise and business, or that of your staff group,
by answering the following questions:*

1) What is the expertise to which you lay claim?

2) What are the products and services you currently possess that use this expertise?

3) What are the business problems facing your clients?

4) How can you use your expertise to build the capacity of your clients to better manage profitability and cost, quality, cycle time, and unique customer response?

5) What techniques and methodologies will help your clients solve their business problems?

6) What expertise, techniques and methodologies are you currently lacking that could help your clients? Where/how can you access or acquire them?

7) What techniques and methodologies are no longer directly relevant to solving your clients' problems?

8) Who is your competition? What makes them attractive to your client?

9) What makes your offer unique and different from your competition?

10) Who are your bankers? What is the promise they want?

11) What are the most difficult issues that exist between you and your client **and** you and your bankers?

# Chapter Three

## Determining Relevance, Timeliness and Fit

# Concept

## *RELEVANCE*

- Is there a match between your expertise and what is needed to build client capacity?

- Can your expertise build capacity in this unit?

- How do you articulate the connection between your expertise and the business of the client unit?

- What is the business argument that supports the application of your expertise?

**No expertise that builds capacity = ~~RELEVANCE~~**


## *TIMELINESS*

- Do people have time and energy to focus on this effort in addition to everything else?

- Is the timing right?

- Are the necessary monies and resources available?

**No time, energy, resources, or focus to support the use of your expertise = ~~TIMELY~~**


## *FIT*

- Is this unit ready and willing to create the conditions for your strategy and expertise to work?

- Is the general disposition of the unit friendly about moving toward what you believe is the best way of operating?

- Is the client willing to take personal action to support that way of operating?

**Client unwilling to do what is necessary for implementation = ~~FIT~~**

# Chapter Four

## Determining Stance

# Concept

## Determine Your Stance

**Definition:**
...your position or point of view about the best use of your expertise to build client capacity to compete in the marketplace.

Your stance is based on your belief about how organizational power should be used. Fundamentally, you have two choices:

*Consolidation of Power* – Your expertise is best used to create centralized control of business literacy, decision making, resources, information, training, processes, and behaviors. If you believe in consolidating power, you seek ways to increase management control.

*Distribution of Power* – Your expertise is best used to equip core workers with business literacy, resources, information, training, decision making — enabling them to choose accountability for the business — to increase the organization's capacity to compete in the marketplace. If you believe in distributing power, you seek ways to increase core worker knowledge, power, and accountability.

***These stances are not mutually exclusive. They could be thought of as two ends of a continuum. In general, we believe most organizations are overly consolidated and can benefit from increased distribution of power.***

# Application:

**Discover your stance** by asking yourself the following questions:

Do you believe work processes should be controlled by *management* or by those who do the work?

Do you believe that information should be widely and broadly disseminated to all or closely held in the hands of *management*?

Do you believe policies and procedures should be instituted for control or to engender collaboration?

Do you believe the organization structure should ease internal management or administration, or grant ease of access to the customer?

## NEXT:

Make a list of *techniques* or activities in which you or your staff unit have engaged the past month.

Categorize each in the worksheet on the next page.

Place techniques that serve to control, restrict, limit, remove, etc. in the *consolidated* category.

Place techniques that increase learning, core worker decision making, empowerment, employee options, etc. in the *distributed* category.

Examine the patterns and confront your stance.

| Techniques You Use That Consolidate Power | Techniques You Use That Distribute Power |
| --- | --- |
| | |

# Chapter Five

## Creating Powerful Client Offers

# Concept

## Make Powerful Client Offers -

### *Essential Elements:*

√ credible

√ impact quality, profitability, cycle time and unique customer response

√ compelling

√ promise results

√ backed by a guarantee

### *Key Questions:*

1) How does your expertise in Human Resources, Finance, Information Systems, etc. impact business results?

2) What is the best use of your expertise (STANCE) for building your client's capacity to compete in the marketplace?

3) What is your promise of results from using your expertise and what guarantee are you willing to make to fulfill your promise?

*Sample Offers:*

*Human Resources -*

"**Our expertise is the ability to** organize people to get work done. **By** redesigning certain jobs we can help get the product through the line faster. **If we haven't delivered** the business changes we promised within six months, we will search and find another consultant who can do the work that needs to be done and we will pay for it out of our own budget."

*Finance -*

"**My expertise is the ability to** create useful financial measures and increase financial understanding in order to make good business decisions. **By** consulting and training in this area I can help reduce costs and increase output. **If I can't accomplish improvement** in these areas in four months, I'll gladly support your approach and help you implement it at no cost to you."

*Information Systems -*

"**Our expertise is in the ability to** retrieve, manipulate and distribute information in ways that create business literacy and allow good decision making at all levels. **By** providing core workers with options in how they respond to customers, we can create unique response in the marketplace. **If you provide the conditions we request and we can't deliver**, we will agree, at our own time and expense, to learn what we need to make it work."

# Application

## Creating an offer:

Complete the sentences for each element of your offer. Use the examples below and the *Sample Offers* from the previous page as guides.

### [what] My expertise is (the ability to) ...
My expertise is the ability to create learning solutions to enable better employee decision making and performance.

_____

_____

_____

_____

### [how] By ...
By helping workers learn how to serve customers effectively, we can increase customer satisfaction ratings and customer retention levels (by X%).

_____

_____

_____

_____

### [consequence] If ...
If satisfaction ratings fail to improve and retention doesn't increase (by X amount) in four months, I'll pay for an external consultant out of my budget to help you get the results I promised.

_____

_____

_____

_____

# Tool

## Assess the Strength of Your Offer:

1. What makes it unique in the marketplace (in your client's eyes)?

2. How does it promise to solve a problem or address an issue that directly impacts quality, profitability, cycle time and/or unique customer response?

3. What are the promises you are making; what are the guarantees you are offering?

4. How does your offer build your client's capacity to compete?

*Use the worksheets to assess the strength of your offer in the marketplace.*

Ask:

How is your market position?
Is there room for growth?
How do you stack up against external competitors?

Work through this analysis and consider what it all means in terms of your vulnerability and strategic requirements.

# *Example of HR Staff Chart*

## <u>HR</u> Staff Market Analysis

| FACTOR | ME OR MY STAFF GROUP | COMPETITOR #1 | COMPETITOR #2 |
|---|---|---|---|
| Gross Revenue | $200,000 | Unclear | $200,000 |
| -Expenses | $6,000 | $55,000 | $24,000 |
| = PROFIT | $194,000 | Unknown | $156,000 |
| PRIMARY OFFER TO CLIENTS | get work group functioning | increase retention | get work group functioning |
| HOW OFFER IS UNIQUE TO MARKETPLACE | outcome driven | unique processes | outcome driven |
| HOW OFFER IS COMPELLING TO CLIENTS | solves problem impacting business results | solves ongoing problem | solves problem impacting business results |
| RELEVANCE OF OFFER TO CLIENT BOTTOM LINE | success adds $194,000 to profit | success improves productivity | success adds $156,000 to profit |
| MARKET STRENGTHS | history of successes | reputation, marketing | established name, a lot of resources |
| MARKET WEAKNESSES | lack of client confidence | focuses on activity more than result | ??? |
| SERVICE GUARANTEES | pay for external consultants | none | satisfaction only |

# _____ Staff Market Analysis

| FACTOR | ME OR MY STAFF GROUP | COMPETITOR #1 | COMPETITOR #2 |
|---|---|---|---|
| Gross Revenue | 1 | 1 | 1 |
| -Expenses | 2 | 2 | 2 |
| = PROFIT | 3 | 3 | 3 |
| PRIMARY OFFER TO CLIENTS | | | |
| HOW OFFER IS UNIQUE TO MARKETPLACE | | | |
| HOW OFFER IS COMPELLING TO CLIENTS | | | |
| RELEVANCE OF OFFER TO CLIENT BOTTOM LINE | 4 | 4 | 4 |
| MARKET STRENGTHS | | | |
| MARKET WEAKNESSES | | | |
| SERVICE GUARANTEES | | | |

1 Business Impact
2 Budget + Oth Exp
3 NET VALUE ADDED
4 Impact on quality, profitability, cycle time and/or unique response to customer

# Chapter Six

## Managing Entry Requirements

# Concept

## 3 Ways to Enter the Client Organization:

### *Client Calls Consultant –*

Client initiates interaction.

Do not assume client assessments and solutions are right; Perform your own *discovery* prior to *implementation*.

### *Consultant Calls Client –*

You initiate contact with them.

Express willingness to make promises if you find your expertise is relevant.

Don't assume you are relevant and have solutions until *discovery* is complete.

### *Mandated Entry –*

Something occurs that requires a meeting between you and the client (i.e. corporate program, manager demand, regulatory requirement).

Make sure everyone understands that it is a mandate.

*Some Rules For Effective Contracting With A Mandated Entry*

**Don't:**

- √ Assume that it is not necessary to do *Contracting* and *Discovery*

- √ Assume a mandate will be implemented the same way in each unit

- √ Assume that your expertise will be utilized the same way in each unit

- √ Approach the situation as the agent of the mandator

- √ Assume that now is the right time for implementing the mandate

**Do:**

- √ Contract with your manager (banker/mandator) prior to meeting with the client, if possible

- √ Make sure everyone involved is clear about the mandate

- √ Be aware of the potential necessity to include others in the *Contracting* meeting

- √ Apply the consulting model to the situation

- √ Pay attention to the emotional issues generated by the mandate by both you and your client

- √ Expect some client resistance

# Chapter Seven

## Contracting with Purpose

# Concept

## Contracting Stage

**Purpose:**

To **create the conditions** necessary to assess the relevance, timeliness and fit of your expertise.

**Goals:**

To establish an agreement and working relationship that will allow you to discover if your expertise is relevant, timely and fits.

**Outcomes:**

√ Establish who your "real" client is

√ Get your client's view of the situation

√ Find out what your client wants from you

√ Negotiate your essential wants for testing *relevance, timeliness and fit*

√ Deal directly with issues of control, vulnerability and trust in both of you

√ Extend and establish goodwill with your client

√ Agree on proceeding to the *Discovery* stage

# Tool

*Following are three models for contracting with a client. With the exception of steps specific to a mandate, client-initiated and consultant-initiated contracting follow the same essential steps.*

## Steps of a CLIENT INITIATED Contracting Meeting

| Step 1 | Make personal contact |
|--------|----------------------|
| Step 2 | Ask client for their view of the meeting's purpose |
| Step 3 | Extend understanding |
| Step 4 | Ask client for their wants |
| Step 5 | Tell the client your wants:<br><br>• freedom to develop your own viewpoint<br>• access to information in the unit<br>• freedom to raise difficult issues<br>• interviewee confidentiality |
| Step 6 | Be prepared to give business reasons for your wants (To assess Relevance, Timeliness and Fit) |
| Step 7 | Come to an agreement on the wants |
| Step 8 | Acknowledge the client's contribution to the success of the meeting |
| Step 9 | Restate the agreements |

# Steps of a CONSULTANT INITIATED Contracting Meeting

| Step 1 | Make personal contact |
| --- | --- |
| Step 2 | Acknowledge the initiation and make the offer to client |
| Step 3 | Ask client what contribution they think you can make |
| Step 4 | Extend understanding |
| Step 5 | Ask client for their wants |
| Step 6 | Tell the client your wants:<br><br>• freedom to develop your own viewpoint<br>• access to information in the unit<br>• freedom to raise difficult issues<br>• interviewee confidentiality |
| Step 7 | Be prepared to give business reasons for your wants (Relevance, Timeliness, Fit) |
| Step 8 | Come to an agreement on the wants |
| Step 9 | Acknowledge the client's contribution to the success of the meeting |
| Step 10 | Restate the agreements |

## Steps of a MANDATED Contracting Meeting

| Step 1 | Make personal contact |
|---|---|
| Step 2 | Acknowledge the mandate |
| Step 3 | Ask client for concerns and acknowledge them |
| Step 4 | Ask client for their view of the meeting's purpose |
| Step 5 | Extend understanding |
| Step 6 | Ask client for their wants |
| Step 7 | Tell the client your wants:<br><br>• freedom to develop your own viewpoint<br>• access to information in the unit<br>• freedom to raise difficult issues<br>• interviewee confidentiality |
| Step 8 | Be prepared to give business reasons for your wants (Relevance, Timeliness, Fit) |
| Step 9 | Come to an agreement on the wants |
| Step 10 | Acknowledge the client's contribution to the success of the meeting |
| Step 11 | Restate the agreements |

# Application

**Contracting Meeting Worksheet Sample**
**Steps 1-5**

| | **Meeting Steps** | **Example** |
|---|---|---|
| **Step 1** | Make personal contact | I appreciate your willingness to meet and talk about this situation. After learning more about your situation I'll know how, or if, I can help. |
| **Step 2** | Acknowledge the mandate | It's my understanding that we were both told to meet to come up with a solution to this problem. What is your understanding? |
| **Step 3** | Ask client for concerns and acknowledge them | What concerns do you have about working together like this under these circumstances? |
| **Step 4** | Ask client for their view of the meeting's purpose | What do you see as the purpose of today's meeting? |
| **Step 5** | Extend understanding | It sounds like you aren't real hopeful about our ability to succeed based on your past experience. Is that right? |

# Contracting Meeting Worksheet Sample
## Steps 6-11

| | Meeting Steps | Example |
|---|---|---|
| Step 6 | Ask client for their wants | What do you want from me relating to how we work together? ...What else? ...What else? |
| Step 7 | Tell the client your wants:<br><br>• freedom to develop your own viewpoint<br>• access to information in the unit<br>• freedom to raise difficult issues<br>• interviewee confidentiality | There are also some things I want from you to assess how I can be helpful. First, I want the freedom to develop my own point of view about the situation here. How do you feel about that?<br>I will want to meet with approximately twelve people from your department to get some information from their perspective regarding this issue. I want to assure them of confidentiality when we meet. How do you feel about that?<br>Since I have no idea what I'm going to find when I start gathering information, I also want to be able to raise difficult issues with you. How do you feel about me doing that? |
| Step 8 | Be prepared to give business reasons for your wants | I'm asking for these things because as I collect information, I'll be asking myself if my expertise has relevance, timeliness, and fit for resolving this problem. I need to have sufficient information to be able to do that because, ultimately, I want to make a promise for results. |
| Step 9 | Come to an agreement on the wants | So you're okay with me meeting with the twelve people, guaranteeing their confidentiality, raising difficult issues as I see the need, and being free to develop my own point of view about the situation? And I've agreed to meet with you each week to keep you informed on my progress, right? |
| Step 10 | Acknowledge the client's contribution to the success of the meeting | I appreciate your willingness to share your feelings with me openly about this situation and to move forward under some unpleasant circumstances. I think it really helped us get clear about some of the challenges and get off to a good start. |
| Step 11 | Restate the agreements | So you're going to have your secretary get back to me with the names of the twelve people. I'll set up the appointments and you'll send me an email with the location of our next meeting. Is that right? |

# Contracting Meeting Preparation Worksheet

| | **Meeting Steps** | **What I Will Say** |
|---|---|---|
| **Step 1** | Make personal contact | |
| **Step 2** | Acknowledge the mandate | |
| **Step 3** | Ask client for concerns and acknowledge them | |
| **Step 4** | Ask client for their view of the meeting's purpose | |
| **Step 5** | Extend understanding | |
| **Step 6** | Ask client for their wants | |
| **Step 7** | Tell the client your wants:<br>• freedom to develop your own viewpoint<br>• access to information in the unit<br>• freedom to raise difficult issues<br>• interviewee confidentiality | |
| **Step 8** | Be prepared to give business reasons for your wants | |
| **Step 9** | Come to an agreement on the wants | |
| **Step 10** | Acknowledge the client's contribution to the success of the meeting | |
| **Step 11** | Restate the agreements | |

# Tool

## Helpful Tips For Effective Contracting Meetings
**Remember these tips at each step of contracting...**

Step 1 – Bring an attitude of openness and sincere desire to help. Remember that trust and control are always at stake.

Step 2 – Be clear about your understanding of the mandate and how the meeting came about.

Step 3 – Listen and ask for concerns, but don't try to resolve them at this point. Merely acknowledge their existence.

Step 4 – Listen to your client's statement of purpose for the meeting and be prepared to reconcile issues.

Step 5 – Summarize client comments to show your understanding and ask for acknowledgment. Take their side.

Step 6 – Ask for client *wants* prior to stating yours. Probe until you're satisfied they are finished.

Step 7 – State as *wants* the agreements you need from the client to assess relevance. Be clear and concise.

Step 8 – Provide reasonable explanations for your wants including the necessity of assessing the relevance of your expertise as pointed out in Step 7.

Step 9 – Ask directly for agreement on each of your wants.

Step 10 – Express appreciation for the things the client did to make the meeting successful.

Step 11 – Be clear as to what each of you has agreed.

# Chapter Eight

## Conducting Discovery

# Concept

## Quantitative vs Qualitative Data

**Quantitative** data describes *what is occurring* and can assist in pinpointing opportunities to use your expertise to help the business.

**Qualitative** data provides insight into *why things are occurring* — root causes — and may reveal useful solutions to a problem.

**Examples of quantitative data collection techniques:**

√ Surveys

√ Reports

√ Data sheets

**Examples of qualitative data collection techniques:**

√ Focus groups

√ Confidential interviews

√ Observations

# Tool

*The Discovery Model is a way to extract, analyze, and assess information pertaining to a variety of factors influencing organizational behavior related to your client's situation.*

## BASIC STEPS FOR USING THE MODEL:

1) Collect data relating to the organization's social contract, management practices, and organizational architecture.

2) Interpret information according to your stance (i.e. distributed or consolidated).

3) Seek opportunities to leverage your expertise to build client capacity.

4) Assess the opportunities according to relevance, timeliness and fit.

5) Develop a point of view regarding the difficult fit issues.

## Discovery Model

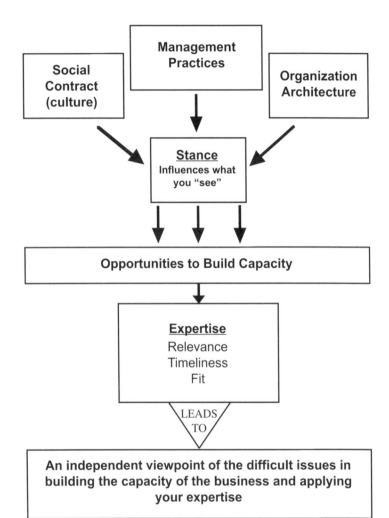

# Concept

### *Guidelines for Gathering Information*

**Don't:**

√ Attempt to problem-solve when collecting data

√ Take sides or form conclusions

√ Constrain the data with yes/no questions

√ Repeat what others have told you in confidence

**Do:**

√ Keep an open mind

√ Remain focused on determining relevance, timeliness and fit

√ Ask open-ended questions

√ Encourage others to talk about what is important to them

√ Probe into issues raised

√ Keep confidences

# Application

## Sample Interview Questions for Discovery

***Social Contract*** *– understanding the nature of the relationship*

**Sample questions** to discover the Social Contract

Who is knowledgable about the business in terms of financial position, budgets, marketplace challenges, operations, and interdependencies?

Who feels personally accountable for the success of the whole business?

Who is responsible for the morale and motivation of employees?

How do you feel about working in this organization?

What do you feel you can personally change?

What are the key measures of success for the organization?

How does work get done in the business?

How does the future of the organization look to you?

When you see a better way to do things, how easy is it to make the changes?

What is your contribution to the problem?

What would others say is your contribution?

***Management Practices*** – *the window to management's stance*

Management practices are generally created for two reasons:

√        To get something done
√        To make the values visible

*Most management practices were created to support the consolidated management stance. If your stance is different, these must be examined and changed if a meaningful shift is to occur.*

Here are some major management practices:

√   Conducting performance reviews

√   Making hiring decisions

√   Convening meetings

√   Changing work processes

√   Managing customer relationships

√   Managing conflict and raising difficult issues

√   Budgeting

**Sample questions** to discover Management Practices
*Of each practice, you may ask the following three questions:*

Who has the responsibility for carrying out this practice?

Can others influence this practice?

In this practice, is managing segregated from the actual work?

---

***Organization Architecture*** *– form follows function*

**Sample questions** to discover Organization Architecture:

JOB DESIGN

Who controls your work?

How is it controlled?

How is your performance measured?

How does what you do relate to your job description?

Are you encouraged to learn new skills and expand your ability to contribute?

Are you encouraged to teach skills you have to others?

Are you encouraged to seek new ways of performing tasks to improve effectiveness?

MANAGEMENT ROLE

Is managing separated from doing the work?

Is management seen as a class of people or a set of tasks?

STAFF ROLE

Who do you think staff groups see as their client?

What does staff see as their mission and purpose?

## REWARDS

Is everyone rewarded based on the unit's performance in the marketplace?

Are rewards focused on the individual or unit performance?

## STRUCTURE

Are people grouped for customer convenience or internal ease of control?

How does the structure support control and consistency?

How does the structure support innovation and unique response?

## Interview Tips

√ Explain the process for gathering information and holding a feedback meeting

√ Disclose agreement about confidentiality

√ Ask probing questions (avoid yes/no questions)

## Four useful catchall questions for the end of the interview

What question should I have asked that I didn't?

If you could change anything in the organization to make things better, what would it be?

What is done so well here that you would not change it regardless of what else you might change?

If you were me trying to help your organization solve this problem, what would you want to know that we haven't talked about?

# Application

## Interview Preparation Worksheets

### *Social Contract Questions*

_____

_____

_____

_____

_____

_____

_____

_____

_____

_____

### *Management Practices Questions*

_____

_____

_____

_____

_____

_____

_____

_____

_____

_____

## Organization Architecture Questions

_____

_____

_____

_____

_____

_____

_____

_____

_____

_____

_____

## Other Questions You Want To Ask

_____

_____

_____

_____

_____

_____

_____

_____

_____

_____

# Chapter Nine

## Sorting and Analyzing Discovery Information

# Concept

## Sorting the Information

### *Objective*

Sort the discovery information so feedback can be presented as:

SIMPLE – self-evident, obvious

CLEAR – without confusion

MANAGEABLE – not overwhelming

ACTIONABLE – can be acted upon

# Application

### Sort for *Relevance* First

1) Specify where your expertise can make a difference in the system.

2) Identify likely results. Show how the intervention you advocate would lead to increased business performance.

3) Suggest effective methods or actions to carry out the intervention.

### Define *Timeliness* Issues

1) Focus – Are there distractions that may hinder success?

2) Time – Is this an effective time for solving the problem?

3) Availability – Will people be able to dedicate appropriate time?

4) Resources – Are the necessary resources available?

### Identify the *Fit* Issues

Consider:

1) Where was your stance not shared?

2) What conditions in the unit would the client have to agree to create in order to support the application of your expertise and methods?

3) In what areas do you and your client appear to agree/disagree on how to build capacity in the unit?

---

## Assess Opportunities

The framework on the next page shows the correlation between *Relevance* and *Fit*. When your expertise has high *Relevance* (meaning your expertise can help the business), client *Fit* issues will be significant (which means the client is not doing what you believe is necessary to get the results). Generally, the greater the *Relevance*, the greater the *Fit* issues. When you have high *Relevance* and significant *Fit* issues — that you are able to resolve — you fall into Quadrant IV where you can create high business impact.

Seek Quadrant IV opportunities. Avoiding *Fit* issues and accepting less relevant opportunities results in less business impact.

## Framework

### Determining Potential Business Impact
### (Relevance-Fit Impact Chart)

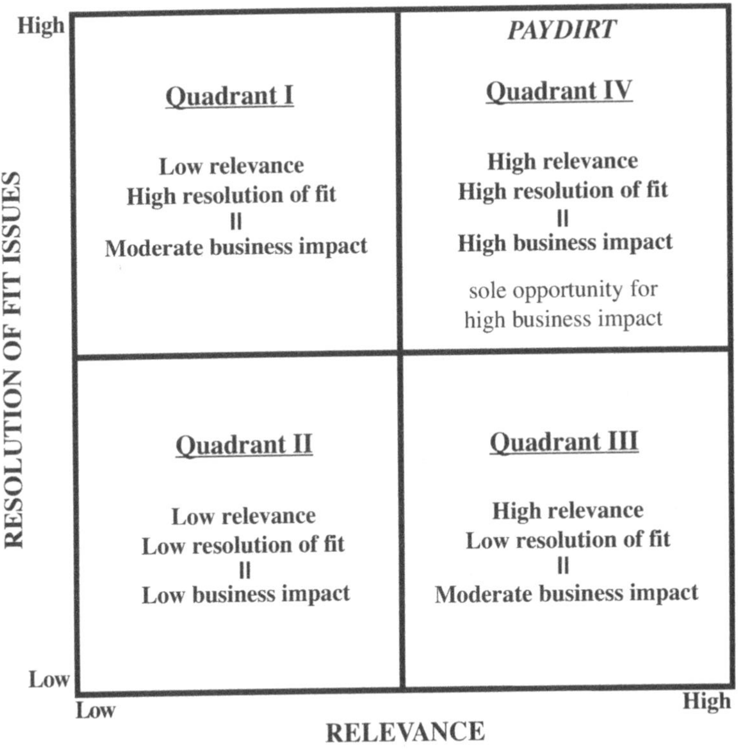

PAYDIRT
Quadrant I
Low relevance
High resolution of fit
=
Moderate business impact
Quadrant IV
High relevance
High resolution of fit
=
High business impact
sole opportunity for
high business impact
Quadrant II
Low relevance
Low resolution of fit
=
Low business impact
Quadrant III
High relevance
Low resolution of fit
=
Moderate business impact
RESOLUTION OF FIT ISSUES
High
Low
RELEVANCE
Low
High

## Evaluate Potential Recommendations

Here is a tool to help you and your clients analyze recommendations according to *Results, Speed, Cost* and *Effort*.

An option that scores LOW on results is usually rejected as too weak to be worth pursuing. An option that yields HIGH results at HIGH speed (quickly) requiring LOW cost and LOW effort may provide an excellent opportunity to build business capacity. These are considered *quick hits* or *no-brainers*. All other combinations should be weighed and considered in the context of strategy and relevance to the marketplace.

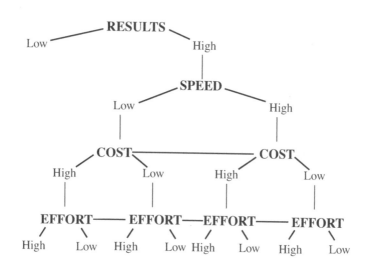

Completed charts are provided on the following pages as examples for using the tool.

### *See Example 1*:

1) List each of your recommendations as *options* along the left-hand column of the Initiative Prioritization Chart.
2) Determine if the criteria listed across the top are appropriate to your client's situation. If not, add to the list or substitute as necessary.
3) If criteria are not equally important, weight them. The more important the criterion, the greater the multiplier.
4) When assessing each option, rate them on a scale of 0-10 with 10 being most favorable. Please note that the rating is always high when the direction is favorable (i.e. LOW cost, LOW effort, or HIGH results all receive high ratings such as a 9 or 10). After you rate options on each criterion, multiply each rating by its weight factor and enter the result in the appropriate box.
5) Add across to obtain a total score for each option. Generally speaking, the best choice is the option with the highest total score.

### *See Example 2*:

Alternatively, you may wish to enter raw values for each unweighted criteria without adding across for a total score. This provides a useful visual comparison of strengths and weaknesses, and a quick assessment of options.

# Application

## Initiative Prioritization Chart

### Example 1

|          | Speed x 2 | Cost x 2 | Effort x 1 | Results x 3 | TOTAL |
|----------|-----------|----------|------------|-------------|-------|
| Option 1 | 16        | 6        | 6          | 15          | 43    |
| Option 2 | 4         | 8        | 3          | 15          | 30    |
| Option 3 | 12        | 20       | 7          | 21          | 60    |
| Option 4 | 10        | 14       | 4          | 18          | 46    |
| Option 5 | 14        | 20       | 5          | 15          | 54    |

calculation:

8(speed rating) x 2(weighted factor) = 16

**SPEED** of implementation
0 1 2 3 4 5 6 7 8 9 10
low                high

**COST** of implementation
0 1 2 3 4 5 6 7 8 9 10
high                low

**EFFORT** required
0 1 2 3 4 5 6 7 8 9 10
high                low

**RESULTS** anticipated
0 1 2 3 4 5 6 7 8 9 10
low                high

In the example above, SPEED is rated at 8 because Option 1 can be implemented rather quickly. We multiply 8 by 2 (the weight given to the SPEED factor) and enter 16. Option 3 has the greatest total score of 60 which means it may provide the best opportunity for building capacity.

# Initiative Prioritization Chart

## Example 2

| | Speed | Cost | Effort | Results | TOTAL |
|---|---|---|---|---|---|
| **Option 1** | (9) | (6) | 7 | (9) | |
| **Option 2** | 2 | 2 | (8) | 5 | |
| **Option 3** | 7 | (6) | 6 | 4 | |
| **Option 4** | 4 | 3 | 4 | 5 | |
| **Option 5** | 8 | 2 | 4 | 6 | |

**SPEED** of implementation      0 1 2 3 4 5 6 7 8 (9) 10
       low      high

**COST** of implementation      0 1 2 3 4 5 6 7 8 9 10
       high      low

**EFFORT** required      0 1 2 3 4 5 6 7 8 9 10
       high      low

**RESULTS** anticipated      0 1 2 3 4 5 6 7 8 9 10
       low      high

Circled numbers represent the high score for each column and provide a useful visual comparison of strengths and weaknesses. This may be particularly useful when criteria are of equal value and you need a quick assessment of options. In our example, three of the highest ratings fall in Option 1 suggesting that it may be the strongest option to consider.

**Tool**

## Initiative Prioritization Chart

| | Speed x | Cost x | Effort x | Results x | TOTAL |
|---|---|---|---|---|---|
| Opt 1 | | | | | |
| Opt 2 | | | | | |
| Opt 3 | | | | | |
| Opt 4 | | | | | |
| Opt 5 | | | | | |

| | Speed | Cost | Effort | Results | TOTAL |
|---|---|---|---|---|---|
| Opt 1 | | | | | |
| Opt 2 | | | | | |
| Opt 3 | | | | | |
| Opt 4 | | | | | |
| Opt 5 | | | | | |

# Chapter Ten

## Conducting the Feedback Meeting

# Concept

## The Feedback Meeting

**Objectives:**

The purpose of the feedback meeting is to discuss *Relevance*, *Timeliness* and *Fit* with particular focus on framing *Fit* when expertise is relevant.

√ Resolving and negotiating *Fit* to obtain a go/no-go decision

√ Contracting for ongoing implementation

There are two phases in the feedback meeting:

The first phase confronts the *Fit* issues and accomplishes a decision regarding whether or not to accept recommendations and begin implementation.

The second phase serves to establish the relationship for implementation. Both phases are essential for ensuring success.

# Steps for a Client Feedback Meeting (Phase 1)

| | |
|---|---|
| **Step 1** | Make personal contact |
| **Step 2** | Review agreements from contracting meeting |
| **Step 3** | State the agenda for this meeting |
| **Step 4** | Give good faith statement about relevance and timeliness |
| **Step 5** | Focus the discussion on FIT |
| **Step 6** | Frame the FIT issue:<br>• give the business reasons for your stance<br>• reference the information<br>• briefly present recommendations |
| **Step 7** | Confront the client with a choice |
| **Step 8** | Contract with client on "Fit conditions" to support your expertise |
| **Step 9** | Negotiate application of your expertise and close the meeting:<br>• intervention/outcome<br>• promises/guarantees<br>• consequences |

**The Feedback Meeting Model (Phase 1)**
**Frame the Meeting; Present the Feedback**
**(Steps 1-4)**

**Step 1:** Make personal contact

- Choose for goodwill and assume the same in your client.

- Trust and control are still at stake.


**Step 2:** Review the contract

- Remind client what was agreed to at the contracting meeting –
an agreement to:
    - develop an independent viewpoint
    - access information
    - raise difficult issues
    - ensure interviewee confidentiality

- Restate what you were assessing (the Relevance, Timeliness and
Fit of your expertise).


**Step 3:** State the agenda/frame for this meeting.

- Outline your intentions for the meeting.


**Step 4:** Give good faith statements about relevance and timeliness

- State where your expertise could have impact.

- Summarize timeliness - necessary time and money.

---

# Application

*Frame the Meeting; Present the Feedback* - **Worksheet Sample**

| **Feedback Meeting Steps** | | **Example** |
|---|---|---|
| **Step 1** | Make personal contact | I appreciate this opportunity to discuss with you what I learned. We'll discuss some of the positive things happening here as well as some of the opportunities. |
| **Step 2** | Review the contract | When we first met, I explained that in the Discovery process, I would be trying to assess relevance, timeliness and fit of my expertise. In order to do so we agreed that I would have access to people to conduct interviews and that those people would be assured confidentiality. We also agreed that I would have the freedom to develop an independent point of view and be able to raise difficult issues. |
| **Step 3** | State the agenda/frame for this meeting | We found several things, but would like to focus the meeting on only a few. |
| **Step 4** | Give good faith statements about relevance and timeliness | We think that the areas of personal accountability and business literacy are where our expertise can make the biggest and most immediate impact on business outcomes. We believe that this is the right time to address these issues and that the available resources are adequate. |

**The Feedback Meeting Model (Phase 1) continued**
**Frame the Fit Issues**
**(Steps 5-6)**

**Step 5:** Focus the discussion on Fit.

• Briefly state that the issue is "Fit" – the willingness of the unit to create conditions for success.

**Step 6:** Frame the Fit issues.

• Give the business reasons for your stance:
Consider what the business case is for wider distribution or consolidation of accountability, literacy, choice, capacity, resources and competence, as it relates to your expertise within this unit.

• Reference the information.
Determine what information you want to refer to here.

• Present recommendations concisely.

# Application continued

*Frame the Fit Issues* - **Worksheet Sample**

| **Feedback Meeting Steps** | | **Example** |
|---|---|---|
| **Step 5** | Focus the discussion on Fit | The issue for the work unit is Fit — the willingness of the unit to do things differently to create conditions for success. |
| **Step 6** | Frame the Fit issues | Here's the way I see the Fit issue: The data revealed a strong preference for self-preservation and information control. It results in turf battles and petty bickering. There is also widespread ignorance as to the impact the unit members have on each other. We believe that distribution of information while focusing on accountability for the whole will improve your ability to meet your productivity goals. |

**Step 7:** Confront the client with the choice about their willingness to create appropriate conditions to fully utilize your expertise.

- Once you frame the choice for the client, leave it alone. Let the client make a choice.

- Do not sell the idea, argue, or make a deal; Do not push for cosmetic agreement.

- Tension indicates consideration of the choice. Do not break the tension; Let the client wrestle with it.

- Test for authenticity of the choice.

    This is a moment of risk. If the client says 'no,' then the meeting is essentially over. As a consultant committed to building capacity in the organization, you cannot make any promises that your expertise, even if used, will make a difference without the client creating appropriate conditions. Without agreeing on fit issues, proceeding would be a waste of time. In fact, proceeding would amount to you taking responsibility for your client's success without conditions to support it.

**Step 8:** Contract with client on "Fit conditions" to support your technology.

- The Feedback Meeting is aimed at a contract as well as a choice.

    You and the client must come to agreement around the conditions that need to be put into place by the client to support your technology.

    Be clear in your own mind what you must have to be effective versus what you would like to have. Compromising the conditions compromises your ability to deliver.

# Application continued

*Confront the Choice; Contract the Fit Conditions -*
**Worksheet Sample**

| Feedback Meeting Steps | | Example |
|---|---|---|
| **Step 7** | Confront the client with the choice | You are going to have to make a choice about the direction in which this organization will go. You will have to let go of some practices that have served you well in the past and take accountability for those choices. Are you willing to move toward widespread business literacy and greater flexibility for work units to make decisions? |
| **Step 8** | Contract with client on "Fit conditions" to support your technology | In order to make this work, you are going to have to be willing to create widespread literacy by sharing information broadly. It also means you will have to be willing to change your focus from internal competition to that of building an integrated team with greater choice and accountability. How do you feel about that? |

**The Feedback Meeting Model (Phase 1) continued**
**Negotiate Promises, Guarantees and Consequences**
**(Step 9)**

**Step 9:** Negotiate the application of your expertise.

- Propose an intervention

- Make promises

- Describe your guarantee

- Clarify your consequences if you fail to deliver

# Application continued

*Negotiate Promises, Guarantees and Consequences -*
**Worksheet Sample**

| **Feedback Meeting Steps** | | **Example** |
|---|---|---|
| **Step 9** | Negotiate the application of your expertise | I propose we set up training programs and multi-literacy sessions to create broad understanding of the business and responsibilities of workgroup members. We will need to do a two-day offsite session with the entire workgroup to resolve the intergroup conflicts. Last, I will provide coaching to the unit leaders to address practices that fail to support employees choosing personal accountability. How do you feel about that? My commitment to you is that, as an outcome of this work, you can expect profitability to improve significantly. To show my sincerity in this, I am willing to put something at risk. If we do everything that's being proposed and it fails to produce the results, I will pay from my budget the fees for an external consultant to solve these problems. How do you feel about that? ...Thank you for a great meeting! I look forward to getting started next week! |

### *Frame the Meeting; Present the Feedback* - Worksheet

| **Feedback Meeting Steps** | | **What I Will Say** |
|---|---|---|
| **Step 1** | Make personal contact | |
| **Step 2** | Review the contract | |
| **Step 3** | State the agenda/frame for this meeting | |
| **Step 4** | Give good faith statements about relevance and timeliness | |

## *Frame the Fit Issues* - **Worksheet**

| **Feedback Meeting Steps** | | **What I Will Say** |
| --- | --- | --- |
| Step 5 | Focus the discussion on Fit | |
| Step 6 | Frame the Fit issue | |

## *Confront the Choice; Contract the Fit Conditions -* **Worksheet**

| **Feedback Meeting Steps** | | **What I Will Say** |
|---|---|---|
| **Step 7** | Confront the client with the choice | |
| **Step 8** | Contract with client on "Fit conditions" to support your technology | |

| **Feedback Meeting Steps** | | **What I Will Say** |
|---|---|---|
| **Step 9** | Negotiate the application of your expertise | |

# Concept

**Ongoing Implementation Meeting (Feedback Meeting, Phase 2)**

At this point, you have reached a *go* decision regarding implementation. However, there are still many issues to resolve. The client has agreed to choose implementation and, in principle, confront the fit issues. Now it is time to work out the details as they relate to implementation planning.

This meeting should occur as an extension of the Feedback meeting whether or not it actually takes place as part of the same event.

**Outcomes:**

√     Establish what you will do

√     Establish what the client will do

√     Develop timeframes for the work

√     Negotiate agreements for working together

√     Clarify expectations including deliverables

√     Extend and establish goodwill with the client

# Steps For A Client Feedback Meeting - Ongoing Implementation Meeting Model (Phase 2)

| | |
|---|---|
| **Step 1** | Make personal contact |
| **Step 2** | Review previous agreements and progress |
| **Step 3** | Deal with client reservations and doubts |
| **Step 4** | Extend understanding |
| **Step 5** | Propose next steps |
| **Step 6** | Confront and negotiate fit issues |
| **Step 7** | Ask client for their wants |
| **Step 8** | Tell the client your wants<br>• what the client needs to do<br>• access to people, information, resources<br>• timeframes for completion |
| **Step 9** | Be prepared to give business reasons for your wants<br>• Refer to agreement to proceed |
| **Step 10** | Come to an agreement on wants |
| **Step 11** | Acknowledge the client's contribution to the success of the meeting |
| **Step 12** | Restate the agreements |

# Application

## Ongoing Implementation Meeting - Worksheet Sample
## Steps 1-6

| | **Meeting Steps** | **Example** |
|---|---|---|
| **Step 1** | Make personal contact | I appreciate your commitment to working together to solve this problem. |
| **Step 2** | Review previous agreements and progress | In our previous meeting, you stated your intention to move forward with the recommendations. You were anxious to solve the problems and wanted to get started right away. |
| **Step 3** | Deal with client reservations and doubts | We discussed some of the challenges you expect to experience with implementation. What other concerns do you have about working together on this project? |
| **Step 4** | Extend understanding | So you see that as something that may get in the way. How can we overcome it? Let's be sure to follow your suggestion here so that doesn't become a problem for us. |
| **Step 5** | Propose next steps | We need to get with Susan in IS to set up the flowchart of events. Once we get that set up, you and I can work with her on specific timelines. How does that sound? |
| **Step 6** | Confront and negotiate fit issues | In our previous meeting you said that you saw this as a staff group issue and didn't see the need for you to be involved. I stated to you that you had to be involved at a fairly significant level for this to work. I want you to have as much at stake here as I do so we work as collaborative partners. How do you feel about making that choice? |

## Ongoing Implementation Meeting - Worksheet Sample
## Steps 7-12

| | **Meeting Steps** | **Example** |
|---|---|---|
| **Step 7** | Ask client for their wants | What do you want from me relating to how we work together? ...What else? ...What else? |
| **Step 8** | Tell the client your wants:<br>• what the client needs to do<br>• access to people, information, resources<br>• timeframes for completion | There are some things I want from you to ensure we are successful. I understand that I will be working primarily with Susan. I know that issues will arise that require me to consult with you directly, however. I need to know that I can call you about an issue and resolve it within a few days. How do you feel about that? You may see difficulties internally that we need to address in this process. I want to be sure that you will include me in these discussions. How do you feel about that? |
| **Step 9** | Be prepared to give business reasons for your wants | My experience tells me that we are less likely to succeed if we are not working closely together every step of the way. I don't want to see you waste limited resources pursuing a path that isn't likely to lead to success. |
| **Step 10** | Come to an agreement on the wants | So I've agreed to be accessible by cell phone and you will meet with me or call me back within a few days even if you're traveling. You will let me know anytime you see something that looks like a potential problem in this process. Is that your understanding? |
| **Step 11** | Acknowledge the client's contribution to the success of the meeting | Thank you for a great meeting. Your openness about issues has helped us get clarity on some key actions and will help us move ahead quickly. |
| **Step 12** | Restate the agreements | We've agreed on each others' availability and how we will work together. Each step will take 2 months and we will meet to discuss the status of things after completing each step. I'll call you Monday to get started. Are we clear on everything? |

# Ongoing Implementation Meeting Preparation Worksheet

| **Meeting Steps** | | **What I Will Say** |
|---|---|---|
| **Step 1** | Make personal contact | |
| **Step 2** | Review previous agreements and progress | |
| **Step 3** | Deal with client reservations and doubts | |
| **Step 4** | Extend understanding | |
| **Step 5** | Propose next steps | |
| **Step 6** | Confront and negotiate fit issues | |
| **Step 7** | Ask client for their wants | |
| **Step 8** | Tell the client your wants: <br><br> •what the client needs to do <br> •access to people, information, resources <br> •timeframes for completion | |
| **Step 9** | Be prepared to give business reasons for your wants | |
| **Step 10** | Come to an agreement on the wants | |
| **Step 11** | Acknowledge the client's contribution to the success of the meeting | |
| **Step 12** | Restate the agreements | |

# Troubleshooting Guide

# Common Challenges for Internal Consultants

(You may want to add your own challenges and solutions for future reference)

| Issue | Actions to take |
|---|---|
| 1. The client rejects my offer. | Reconsider your offer from your client's perspective. If you were the client, would the offer be compelling? How powerfully does the content of the offer impact the client's business? Are the promises you are making something the client cares about? Promises of business outcomes backed by a substantial guarantee can certainly enhance an offer. |
| 2. I can't get the client to "buy in" to my programs. | Make yourself a business person first and a staff person second with your priority being to succeed by helping your client succeed. Let your client's expressed business needs drive your priorities by responding to them first. You may be putting *your* priorities ahead of your client's priorities. You may have a tremendous idea that would have a profound impact on the client's bottom line, but your client has other urgent matters. |

| Issue | Actions to take |
|---|---|
| 3. My clients now have choice and refuse to use me for anything. | Learn your client's business and make an offer directly related to it. Tackle problems they care about. Meet with clients and ask them their reasons for not using you. Ask them what it would take for them to give you an opportunity. |
| 4. My bosses (bankers) still see themselves as my primary clients. | The habit of being served is hard to break. Discuss your promises to your banker and clearly specify what you need in order to fulfill your promises (i.e addressing ineffective banker practices.) Request a change from your banker in order to create the value you are promising. |
| 5. Clients want me to perform administrative work for them instead of solving problems. | Revisit your offers and promises for the appropriate use of your expertise making clear what is required in order to deliver on your promises. Explain to your client your stance about the best use of your expertise and how performing administrative functions prevents you from having greater business impact. |

| Issue | Actions to take |
|-------|-----------------|
|       |                 |

| Issue | Actions to take |
| --- | --- |
|  |  |

| Issue | Actions to take |
| --- | --- |
| | |

| Issue | Actions to take |
|---|---|
| | |

| Issue | Actions to take |
| --- | --- |
|  |  |

# About the Authors...

## James D. Showkeir

Jamie has over 25 years experience in education, management and organization development. His work is focused on developing organizations as communities of people where accountability for success is chosen by all. Working in education, nonprofit and large corporations, he treats the organization–its people–as partners in creating powerful personal learning and growth experiences that directly impact business results.

Jamie worked at the Buick/UAW Employee Development Center, TRW, and Ford Motor Company in various management and organization development positions, working extensively in labor-management partnerships and Joint programs. He served as President of the Autism Society of Michigan and has devoted considerable consulting time and energy to a variety of other nonprofit organizations. Jamie was Dean of the School for Managing and Leading Change which provides in-depth, long-term learning experiences where distributing power is the basis for managing, organizing and structuring successful businesses.

Jamie's clients span a variety of commercial markets. They include: First Union, 3M, Ford, Philadelphia Electric Co., Tucson Electric Power, The Miami Herald Publishing Co., Philadelphia Newspapers Inc., San Luis Obispo Herald-Tribune, Knight-Ridder Inc., Hewlett Packard, Benedictine Health System, Cigna, Kaiser-Permanente, Trignon Blue Cross and Blue Shield, Met Life, British Airways, and The FAA.

Jamie's work is grounded in the belief that the individual's life-world experience is the essence of reality. In order for organizations to change the first person experience must be engaged. This engagement requires intentionally distributing organization power and confronting issues of accountability and choice.

**Kevin Herring**

Kevin has nearly twenty years of experience developing high performance organizations and effective leaders, creating workplace cultures of innovation and commitment, and transforming staff groups into consultants that contribute to core business results.

Kevin's accomplishments include success at Magma Copper Company, a textbook phenomenon with a unique union-management partnership and a workforce that consistently set new industry standards for productivity and profitability. At Magma, Kevin consulted to the Lower Kalamazoo leadership team to create a future for the world's largest underground copper mine nearing the end of its existence. Once production began, the Lower Kalamazoo was able to produce at 20% lower cost than the depleting mine and at nearly half the cost of mine production a few years earlier.

Kevin has held management positions within Fortune 500 companies and consulted to organizations in manufacturing, mining, service, health care,technology, utilities, education and government.

Kevin earned a Master of Arts degree in Organizational Behavior from the University of Illinois along with Bachelor of Arts degrees in Industrial/Organizational Psychology and Japanese from the University of Minnesota.

Kevin's education and experience have taught him to believe that each organization exists not as a sterile, corporeal entity, but as a collection of individuals arranged into social systems to effectively respond to the demands of a marketplace. The essence of Kevin's work in transforming organizations is to create more profitable businesses through practices and work processes that enable employee commitment and effectiveness.